ANIMAL CLOWNS

Does this relaxed orangutan make you want to smile?

by Jane R. McGoldrick

BOOKS FOR YOUNG EXPLORERS
NATIONAL GEOGRAPHIC SOCIETY

Roar! A big male lion lets out a yell when a cub nips him. Although the loud roar may mean "Ouch," the big lion is not hurt. Cubs often play by gently nipping other cubs—and grown-up lions. Only adult male lions have manes, the fluffy hair around their necks.

All lined up, these meerkats seem to be waiting
for a school bus. But they are just letting the sun
warm them. While they rest, they watch for enemies.
A young grizzly bear enjoys the warm sunshine, too.
The playful bear rolls from side to side, reaching for its toes.

The wrinkled face of a moray eel pokes out from a hiding place. Its body is shaped like a snake. The eel slips between rocks underwater and waits for fish to eat. "Oh dear, I forgot to comb my feathers," an emu seems to squawk. The big bird runs fast but cannot fly.

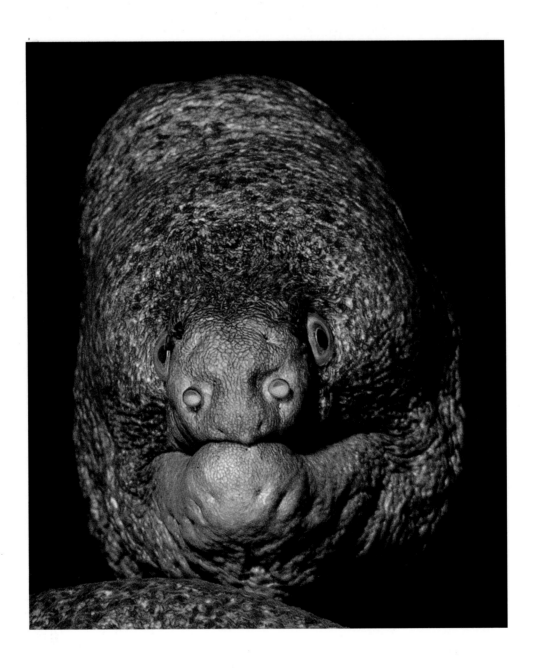

A panda finds a cozy spot in a tree. Would a clown wear a costume that looks like this panda's coat?

If you pretend a little, you can see many animals in circus costumes. The crowned crane has a bright face and neck. Stiff feathers on its head look like a fan. The feathers help it attract another crane for a mate.

A green saddle design helps protect the small saddleback caterpillar. The design warns enemies, such as birds, to watch out. What if a bird still comes near? The caterpillar has stinging spines. If the bird takes a bite, the spines will teach it to stay away!

Look at these funny bills. The toucan uses its big bill to pick fruit or to grab insects and spiders to eat.

This pink bird is called a spoonbill. Its bill is shaped like a spoon with a long handle. To catch fish and other food, the bird swishes its bill from side to side in the water.

The shoebill stork was named for its bill. Some people think the bill looks like a shoe. Do you? The bird uses its bill to feel around in the muddy water for food. Its curved bill seems to give the shoebill a big smile.

A chameleon's tongue is like a jack-in-the-box.
It pops out suddenly. This tongue catches a fly. Usually,
the tongue stays folded inside the chameleon's mouth.
When the lizard sees a meal, the tongue springs out.
The sticky tip grabs the fly, and the tongue springs back

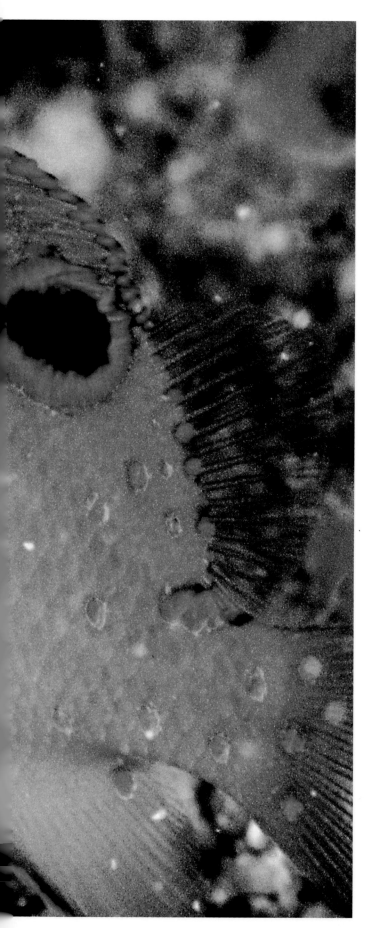

Which spot is the real eye of this young damselfish? It's the spot by the mouth. The other spot is an eyespot. It may confuse an enemy, so the fish can escape.

Big eyes help the night monkey see after dark. At night, it searches for food. It rests during the day.

Animal noses come in many sizes and shapes. This big snout looks a little like an elephant's trunk. It belongs to a male elephant seal. The seal opens his mouth and roars.

You might call this small animal a rabbit with a carrot nose. But bilby is its real name. The bilby uses its snout to sniff and to poke for food.

The star-nosed mole has 22 feelers on its nose. Do you think they make a star shape? The feelers help the mole find food. To eat, the mole moves some of them like fingers.

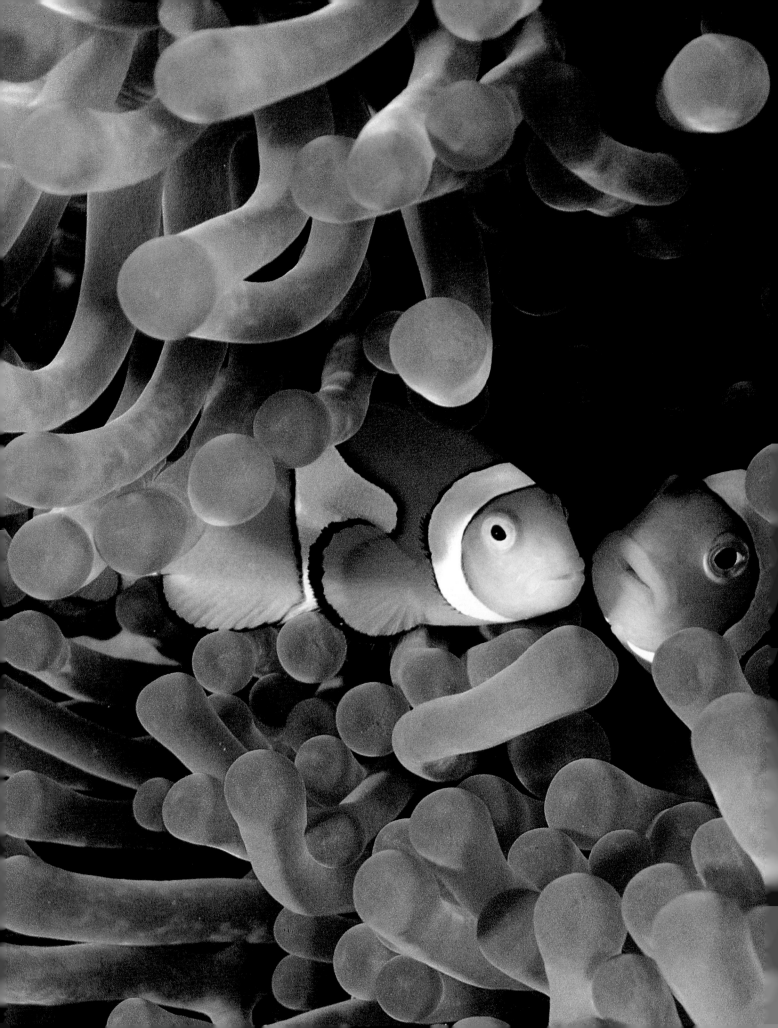

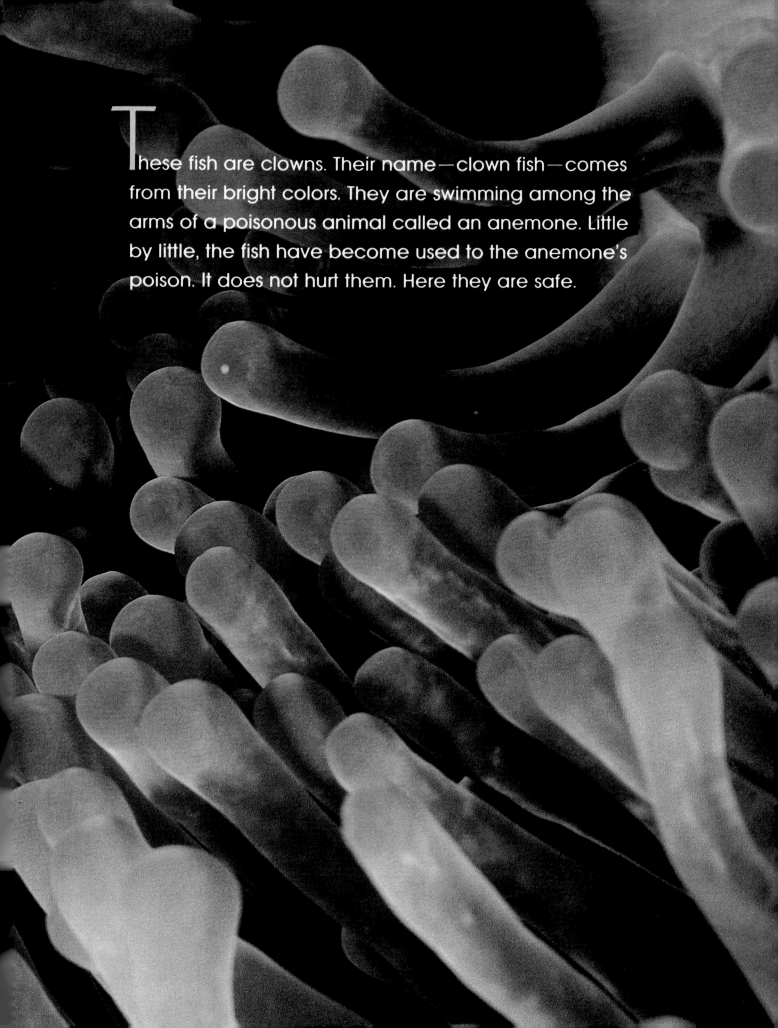

These fish are clowns. Their name—clown fish—comes from their bright colors. They are swimming among the arms of a poisonous animal called an anemone. Little by little, the fish have become used to the anemone's poison. It does not hurt them. Here they are safe.

Once inside the pouch, the joey flips over by turning a somersault. It sticks its head out and looks around.

For many months, this joey was tiny and helpless and couldn't leave its mother's pouch. Now it is big enough to come and go on its own.

A baby kangaroo, called a joey, wants to cuddle up in its mother's pouch. How does it get in?
First, the little kangaroo rests its front paws on the pouch. Next, it pokes its head inside. "It's dark in here," it might be saying.

Adélie penguins dive into icy waters in Antarctica. The birds do not fly. They swim quickly and dive to catch small sea creatures to eat. On the ice, an emperor penguin chick stays warm on its parent's feet.

Two young male giraffes twist their necks together. They push and sway. Two young hippopotamuses rub their jaws. The giraffes and hippos are play-fighting. They do not get hurt. Playing this way may help them learn to protect themselves when they grow up.

The frilled lizard has a collar of skin called a frill. When the lizard feels safe, the frill lies flat. If an enemy comes near, the lizard opens up the frill like an umbrella. Now the lizard looks big and frightening.

This may surprise an enemy so that it stands still for a moment. Then the lizard may have enough time to turn and run away.

These animals seem to have built-in balloons. The male frigatebird blows up a big red sac on his throat to attract a mate. An ape called a siamang puffs up a throat sac, too. "Hoo, hoo, hoo," he cries. The sac makes the sound louder, warning other siamangs to keep away.

Hanging upside down, a small flying fox eats its dinner. The bat is enjoying a kind of fruit called a fig.

First, the flying fox bites into the fig. Next, it pops the whole fig into its mouth. Both cheeks are stuffed as the bat chews. *Gulp!* The flying fox swallows and then licks its lips. Yum, yum, yum.

A blue-footed booby, a tropical seabird, steps high in a dance. Boobies like this one live on some Pacific islands. This male is trying to attract a mate.

Cover: A red-eyed tree frog clings to a branch. Moist pads on its toes grip surfaces as it climbs in forests in Mexico and Central America.

Published by

The National Geographic Society, Washington, D. C.
Gilbert M. Grosvenor, *President and Chairman of the Board*
Melvin M. Payne, Thomas W. McKnew, *Chairmen Emeritus*
Owen R. Anderson, *Executive Vice President*
Robert L. Breeden, *Senior Vice President,*
  Publications and Educational Media

Prepared by

The Special Publications and School Services Division
Donald J. Crump, *Director*
Philip B. Silcott, *Associate Director*
Bonnie S. Lawrence, *Assistant Director*

Staff for this book

M. Barbara Brownell, *Managing Editor*
Jane H. Buxton, *Consulting Managing Editor*
Thomas B. Powell III, *Illustrations Editor*
Debra A. Antonini, *Assistant Picture Editor and Researcher*
Marianne R. Koszorus, *Art Director*
Victoria Cooper, *Researcher*
Artemis S. Lampathakis, *Illustrations Assistant*
Susan A. Bender, Catherine G. Cruz, Marisa J. Farabelli,
  Lisa A. LaFuria, Sandra F. Lotterman, Eliza C. Morton, Dru
  McLoud Stancampiano, *Staff Assistants*

Engraving, Printing, and Product Manufacture

George V. White, *Director,* and Vincent P. Ryan, *Manager,*
  Manufacturing and Quality Management
David V. Showers, *Production Manager*
Kathleen M. Cirucci, *Production Project Manager*
Carol R. Curtis, *Senior Production Staff Assistant*

Consultants

Dr. Thomas A. Jenssen, Virginia Polytechnic Institute and State
  University; Craig Phillips, Biologist; Dr. Walter S. Sheppard,
  U.S.D.A., Agricultural Research Service, Beneficial Insects
  Laboratory; Dr. George E. Watson, St. Albans School; William
  A. Xanten, Jr., National Zoological Park, Smithsonian Institution,
  Scientific Consultants
Dr. Ine N. Noe, *Educational Consultant*
Dr. Lynda Bush, *Reading Consultant*

Illustrations Credits

M.P.L. Fogden/BRUCE COLEMAN LTD. (cover); COMSTOCK/Russ Kinne (1); Yann Arthus-Bertrand/PETER ARNOLD, INC. (2–3); David MacDonald/OXFORD SCIENTIFIC FILMS (4–5 upper); Erwin and Peggy Bauer (5); Tom Myers (6); M. Timothy O'Keefe/BRUCE COLEMAN INC. (7); Tana Hoban (8); P. Morris © Daily Telegraph Colour Library/ MASTERFILE (9 upper); Peter and Sandy Gregg/IMAGERY (9 lower); Medford Taylor (10 upper); Hans Reinhard/BRUCE COLEMAN LTD (10 lower); Günter Ziesler (11); © Stephen Dalton/THE NATIONAL AUDUBON SOCIETY COLLECTION, PR (12–13); Rudie H. Kuiter/OXFORD SCIENTIFIC FILMS (14–15); Rod Williams/ BRUCE COLEMAN LTD. (15); Günter Ziesler (16); Jean-Paul Ferrero/ARDEA (17 upper); © Rod Planck/THE NATIONAL AUDUBON SOCIETY COLLECTION, PR (17 lower); David Doubilet (18–19); APL/D. & J. Heaton (20–21 all); Christine Carvalho (22–23); Frank S. Todd (23 inset); Günter Ziesler (24); © Tom McHugh/THE NATIONAL AUDUBON SOCIETY COLLECTION, PR (25); Michael P.L. Fogden (26 inset); © Jean-Paul Ferrero/AUSCAPE (26–27); © Tom McHugh/THE NATIONAL AUDUBON SOCIETY COLLECTION, PR. (28); Grant Haist (28–29); Merlin Tuttle/BAT CONSERVATION INTERNATIONAL (30–31 all); Tui De Roy (32).

Library of Congress ⊂IP Data

McGoldrick, Jane R.
  Animal clowns / by Jane R. McGoldrick.
  p.   cm. — (Books for young explorers)
  Includes bibliographical references.
  Summary: Text and photographs present animals in amusing poses.
  ISBN 0-87044-772-6 (regular edition)
  ISBN 0-87044-777-7 (library edition)
  1. Animals—Miscellanea—Juvenile literature.   [1. Animals—
—Miscellanea.]   I. Title.   II. Series.
QL49.M184   1989   89-12736
591—dc20   ⊂IP
                                                                              AC

MORE ABOUT ANIMAL CLOWNS

A lot of animals do things that interest us and intrigue us. Just walk outdoors and you'll find a three-ring circus. A male cardinal flits about, showing off bright red feathers. Fireflies flicker, making the night sparkle. An acrobatic squirrel leaps from tree to tree. Or visit a zoo or marine park at feeding time. You'll see monkeys squabbling over a meal or dolphins gulping fish.

As you watch these and other animals, encourage your child to empathize with them. Their behavior often makes us smile, but it has serious functions, too.

When you look closely at animals in action, you will see examples of major kinds of behavior—feeding, defense, communication, courtship, and care of the young. During mating season, the cardinal's bright display helps him attract a female. The firefly's pattern of blinks helps it find its mate. The squirrel defends itself by scampering away from enemies. The monkeys and dolphins are feeding—a vital behavior. All animals must eat to survive.

The giant panda (8),* from the People's Republic of China, seems never to have its fill of its main food, bamboo. This masked animal may feed for 12 hours a day, consuming up to 85 pounds of the shoots. The star-nosed mole (17)—the only mole that swims to find food— usually hunts on pond and stream floors. The North American animal uses tentacles on its nose to locate fish and other creatures.

Large fruit-eating bats known as flying foxes may appear amusing as they gulp food (30-31). But this feeding habit benefits humans. As the bats fly, they scatter undigested seeds. The seeds that sprout may grow into trees. Scientists say that flying foxes may play a role in keeping rain forests alive in Asia, Africa, Australia, and some islands in the Pacific and Indian Oceans.

Even with its food needs met, an animal has to use another kind of behavior to survive. It must defend itself from being eaten. Defense actions can provide amazing shows. The emu (7), a large Australian bird, runs fast to escape enemies—up to 30 miles an hour. In tropical seas, the moray eel (6) stays and fights. Its sharp teeth inflict a painful bite.

Some creatures come with built-in defenses. The African giraffe (24) has a coat that helps camouflage it. Other animals advertise their presence. The saddleback caterpillar (9), in parts of North America, has a unique design and bristly spines. A bird that bites the spines learns to recognize and avoid the insect.

Though the reef-dwelling clown fish is as colorful as a clown, its defense is far from frivolous. The fish protects itself in its tropical Pacific home through a partnership with the sea anemone (18–19). Most fish would be injured or killed by the anemone's poison. The clown fish, however, builds up immunity to the poison. The fish moves almost constantly from side to side among the tentacles. Scientists think it is coating itself with protective mucus from the anemone. At the same time, the fish's movements seem to keep the anemone calm. Such a partnership, in which two different kinds of animals live together, is called symbiosis.

In this case, both animals benefit from the partnership.

Social animals—those that live in groups—cooperate to defend themselves and their young. Meerkats (4–5), native to southern Africa,

Curious but careful, a boy studies a fur seal pup on an island in the South Atlantic Ocean. He does not touch the pup, for it may nip him. Such encounters help children gain respect for other creatures.

*Numbers in parentheses refer to pages in *Animal Clowns.*

live in groups of 5 to 20. While some rest or find food, others do guard duty. Standing on their hind legs, they watch for enemies, often eagles or jackals. A guard's cry sends the others racing to their burrows.

Whether animals live in groups or alone, they communicate with one another. In Central and South America, the night monkey (15), or douroucouli, lives in a group of mother, father, and young. To exchange information, family members make about 50 different sounds, from squeaks to barks. The orangutan (1), a kind of ape in Borneo and Sumatra, uses various facial expressions and vocal sounds

to "talk." For instance, the adult male announces his presence with a series of loud, long calls.

At courtship and mating time, some animals put on especially noisy acts. On an Antarctic beach where southern elephant seals have gathered, the air fills with loud braying. The sound comes from a male (16) trumpeting to ward off rivals. The sound resonates through his big, inflated nose. With such threats, and by fighting, the male wins the right to mate with groups of females.

Many animals have colorful decorations that help them attract mates of their own species. The toucan's bright bill—about eight inches long—makes the bird (11) stand out in forests in Central and South America. The African crowned crane (9) has a headdress—a crest of bristly feathers. This adds a colorful touch to the crane's elaborate courtship dance. Two cranes mate, then may stay together for life.

After mating, female animals lay eggs or give birth to live young. Animals of many species make caring parents. In Antarctica, emperor penguin parents (23) keep especially busy. After the female lays an egg, the male scoops it onto his feet with his bill. There it stays protected and warm against his brood patch, a fold of feathered belly skin. The female then goes off to find food for herself. For about two months, the male eats nothing, living off body fat. After the egg hatches, the parents take turns cuddling the chick against their brood patches. While the chick sits atop one parent's feet, the other parent finds food for itself and its young.

In Australia, kangaroo joeys need long-term care from their mothers. At birth, the joey is about the size of a quarter. The infant makes its way to its mother's pouch, where it attaches itself to a nipple. There it develops. After several months, it climbs out.

Then it comes and goes, seeking the comfort of the pouch for several weeks more. There's a trick to pouch living. Once the baby has climbed inside, it somersaults into a cozy position (20-21).

Feeding, defense, communication, courtship, and care of the young—though the labels may be unfamiliar to your youngster, the concepts will not be new. As you watch animals together, point out these key elements of behavior.

The study of animal behavior is a science known as ethology. Many ethologists observe animals in the wild, drawing no notice to themselves. Some, such as Merlin Tuttle, also work in outdoor or indoor laboratories. Dr. Tuttle has enhanced our knowledge and appreciation of bats through his careful experiments and vivid photographs. Still, he warns not to interfere with bats—or any wild animals. Only a few bats may have rabies. But the risk is present.

"Don't touch wild animals" is the first lesson for you to teach your young explorer. Worlds of learning then await. In your walk together, you may encounter robins, chipmunks, squirrels, rabbits, butterflies, and more. Shhhh—listen, look, learn, and enjoy.

ADDITIONAL READING

Amazing Animals of Australia. (Washington, D. C., National Geographic Society, 1984). Ages 8 and up.

The Amazing Things Animals Do. (Washington, D. C., National Geographic Society, 1989). Ages 8 and up.

Book of Mammals, 2 vols. (Washington, D. C., National Geographic Society, 1981). Ages 8 and up.

How Animals Behave. (Washington, D. C., National Geographic Society, 1984). Ages 8 and up.

Bat expert Merlin Tuttle feeds a banana to flying fox bats. He has trained bats to fly to him on command. Dr. Tuttle observes bat behavior in the wild and in an indoor laboratory. Years of experience qualify him to handle these wild animals—a job for experts only.

MERLIN D. TUTTLE/BAT CONSERVATION INTERNATIONAL